JEWELRY
FORM AND TECHNIQUE

Photo by Jean Callan King

MICHAEL D. GRANDO

JEWELRY
FORM AND TECHNIQUE

VAN NOSTRAND REINHOLD COMPANY
NEW YORK CINCINNATI TORONTO LONDON MELBOURNE

Acknowledgements:
The following have been of important assistance to the author with regard to
this work: Sterling McIlhany, Joseph B. Rissen, Carol Kramer, Billanti Jewelry
Casting Company, Inc., A & S Gem and Mineral Company, Dr. and Mrs. Steven
Karr, Panatela Grande, R. L. Hainline, M.D., Steven Myers, Richard A. Grando,
Nancy C. Newman, Carol Hymowitz, and many others.

Photos on pages 12, 23, 58, 61, 72, and 73 are by Steven S. Myers; all other photos
appearing in this book are by Joseph Vignone.

Van Nostrand Reinhold Company Regional Offices:
New York   Cincinnati   Chicago   Millbrae   Dallas

Van Nostrand Reinhold Company Foreign Offices:
London   Toronto   Melbourne

Copyright © 1969 by Van Nostrand Reinhold Company
Library of Congress Catalog Card Number 77-90302

Designed by Jean Callan King
Printed by Halliday Lithograph Corporation
Bound by William Marley Company

Published by Van Nostrand Reinhold Company
450 West 33rd Street, New York, N.Y. 10001

Published simultaneously in Canada by
D. Van Nostrand Company (Canada), Ltd.

1 3 5 7 9 11 13 15 16 14 12 10 8 6 4 2

This book is dedicated to the tasks so well defined and explored in the life and works of the late Dr. Carl Gustan Jung.

Three techniques created the ring shown in these photographs. The wax model was constructed and carved, cast in white gold, and oxidized. A 1.76-carat round white diamond was suspended by five prongs over an exactly equal negative space created by frasing.

CONTENTS

8

Sterling silver ring containing a
natural sculptured effect (see page
20 for further description).

JEWELRY AS A COMMUNICATIVE ART FORM

1

Is jewelry something more than decoration or ornamentation? At first appraisal it would appear to be just that. Yet there exist examples of jewelry that have been ornamentation only secondarily. The rings and pendants and baubles of Egypt and other ancient civilizations have a religious content that sets them apart from any attempt by man merely to aggrandize his appearance. The folk craftsmen of primitive societies endeavored to capture something of nature and the cosmos in the execution of each piece of their jewelry. Using the religious motifs common to their beliefs, the craftsmen of numerous societies have expressed the rudiments of their culture through various forms of personal adornment.

In our present technical society, it is not difficult to construe that all jewelry is intended as pure ornament. It is also sadly true that much of the present work in precious stones and metals falls short of its aesthetic potential. Perhaps this is due to the fact that the society in which we live measures the value of jewelry essentially by a monetary scale rather than by an artistic one, which leads, of course, to a lessening of the aesthetic ideal.

Sculptural adornment is the result of the artist-craftsman applying to traditional (or in some cases, nontraditional) materials the same concepts and forms that are embodied in the art of sculpture. Within the realm of sculptural adornment, however, one finds certain functional requirements which are not ordinarily encountered by the sculptor. A ring, for example, must be worn on the finger or, more rarely, on the toe. Therefore, a predetermined function is established from the outset. The concept of creating sculpture to be worn may present limitations to some artists, but, for those who can accept this limitation as a challenge and a discipline, there is a continual stimulus of ideas growing from the nature of the function which the form must follow and from the wellspring of creative imagery.

In my own work, sculptural adornment is not only intended to be beautiful or to be admired, it is intended to communicate something of a personal nature as well. Occasionally, I have been able to consult with the individual for whom a piece is being executed. This has provided me with the opportunity to express through that piece something of the nature of the personality for whom it is intended.

As an art form, jewelry must adhere to the principles of communication. That any person may not specifically understand the nature of a given piece of work is not important. The concern of the artist is not with the interpretation or explanation of his work, but with the statement itself. The function of the artist is to remain faithful to his vision, for, while he is the creator, he is, moreover, the instrument or vehicle of creativity. His intent must be meaningful, and that intent must be realized within the work, or any attempt to communicate through the form is futile.

The pure technology of our present society seems to be absent in my own work. Yet upon closer scrutiny of the elements with which I work, I can conclude that no artist is untouched by that which has preceded him. This applies not only to his contact with creative art forms, but to his direct awareness of the technical aids to living, manufacturing, tele-communication, space travel — to the whole stockpile of technical objects and means designed to augment the proficiency of man in coping with his environment.

One of the reasons that people think of jewelry as a craft rather than an art form has to do with the way in which contemporary jewelers serve present-day needs of supply and demand. (They supply the least aesthetic quality for what is a misunderstood demand.) Jewelers are, for the most part, craftsmen and not artists. This does not mean that their marvelous craft, with its nearly alchemical lore and history, cannot be a useful, virile, and needed means of creative expression. However, jewelers today are operating under the same technical pressures as are all other craftsmen and businessmen and are therefore dictated to in varying degrees by the technical and economic aspects of the trade. For example, gold and silver may be purchased from the refinery in sheets, rods, tubes, circles, assorted shapes, carats, etc., and I am convinced that the inorganic, sterile styles of most commonly manufactured jewelry is due to the hard-edged, predictable, unwrought quality of the metals as they are usually purchased for use. Perhaps it is also the sterile attitude many professional jewelers bring to their work for a conditioned consumer public. Whatever the reasons, it seems foolish to allow superb technological advances in what is one of the most ancient of professions to demean, rather than to enhance, the contributions of its practitioners.

Most jewelers have their own method of technical operation which distinguishes them from others in the trade. Yet it is extremely rare that any commercial contemporary work can be recognized as a particular jeweler's style, unless it is recognized through a hallmark employed to identify the maker. In the United States, it is uncommon to find a jeweler who literally signs his work. There are exceptions: some jewelers do work in a hand-wrought, aesthetically developed style, and are involved in the pursuit of the craft on a level of individual creativity. But far too few have evolved a meaningful, unique style, and the sadly neglected custom of the hallmark seems significant in this regard. A signed piece should be indicative of a critical pride in one's work.

Within the years following the Second World War, it appeared that enormous technical achievements were responsible for creating a wave of individual craftsmen bent on reviving old customs associated with their various fields of endeavor. It seemed that the vanishing craftsmen were suddenly rejuvenated by the demand of society for individuality and care in the making of articles for daily use. Now this tendency seems to have waned.

I have heard it argued that jewelry is only a craft, no matter what one may bring to it or how hard one may try to elevate it to another level of expression. This argument has been presented in craft courses offered in many colleges throughout the country. And what an unfortunate teaching when one takes into account the works of innumerable artists which stand as an immutable contradiction to such callous misunderstanding of the criteria of art!

Jewelry should not only be worn as ornament, but should present a totality of thought, mood, and feeling, made meaningful through the use of form, line, mass, texture, color, and style. Using the design elements significantly, it becomes possible to elevate ornament to art.

Left—Necklace composed of semi-precious stone beads, antique "millefiore" beads, and pieces of sterling silver shaped like charms and amulets. *Right*—Necklace of sterling silver, amber beads, stone beads, and ancient Egyptian "faience" beads. In designing these necklaces, metal (sterling silver) and assorted semi-precious stones and beads were combined to relate closely to human anatomy and to explore color, line, mass, and texture. The creative impetus for these objects is totally unconscious in nature. (See pages 23 and 60 for description of rings.)

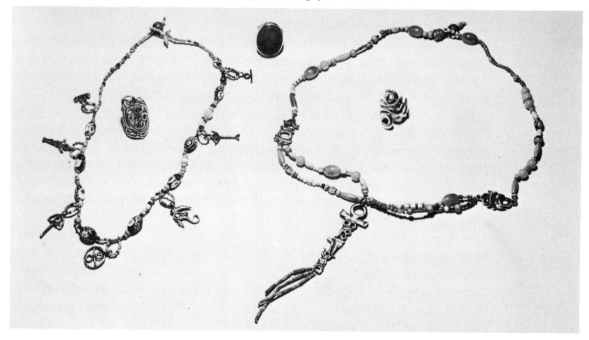

FORMS

2

My own work in recent years has tended to break down into several categories of style. One of these is the mechano-organic style, which manifests itself in mass and motions, and, while remaining within the necessarily limited scale of body adornment, is essentially able to function sculpturally. The work is an object to be worn, but also to be seen and felt as sculpture.

The organic elements of this style are those which seem to resemble living material. The shapes are growing or decaying and are, undeniably, plant, animal, or fungus-like in appearance. This concept of form is dynamic, suggesting energy, a regeneration of life forces, as manifested in pod-like forms or myriad other associations, readily recognizable.

The mechanical elements of this style are not actual working devices, nor do they perform real tasks, as their various gears, cogs, wheels, and parts would seem to indicate. Nevertheless, such elements are at times clearly defined and are, in other instances, subtly suggestive of the mechanical.

When I am working in this particular style, I often find it difficult to predetermine the exact appearance of the finished object. Spontaneity is of

Sterling silver coat pin, centrifugal casting (1966). This pin combines growing and decaying phases of the organic style with some of the device-like forms of the mechanical. Often there is a clear demarcation between these two elements, but in this pin they are fully integrated and therefore less obvious to the eye. The combination of the styles results in a constructed rather than a carved effect.

prime importance and my work seems to evolve from considering the function of the piece, the possibility of using certain stones, and my own flight of imagination.

In many cases, the materials utilized seem to dictate the form of the given object. A stone, for example, may exert an influence on my psyche. It may

14

suggest a mood or feeling that will become evident in my work. The color of the stone may determine the shape of the setting, or the size of the stone may dictate a scale, finished size, and arrangement of metal, form and stone, to which I may be completely oblivious intellectually. Often, it is only upon completion of the jewelry that I become aware of the power of the materials in influencing the form of the finished object.

Left: Sterling silver little-finger ring, set with a 25-carat Russian lapis lazuli (1967). All parts of this "growing form" ring, including the bezel, were executed at the same time by centrifugal casting. The stone is gypsy set (see Chapter 5). *Right:* Sterling silver ring, set with a 40-carat Russian lapis lazuli. This was intended as a masculine mate for the more feminine sterling silver and lapis lazuli ring.

The majority of jewelers today assign a rather secondary place to the setting. The stone has come to be of primary importance. It is possible, however, to view the metal or setting as not merely a device for affixing a pleasing piece of material to the human anatomy but rather as an "environment" for the stone, so that both setting and stone assume equal importance when the work is viewed as a whole. There are no hard and fast rules on how best to provide for an integrated environment for a stone. As you become acquainted with technique, learn temperature data, develop an understanding of metals and materials, the names and uses of tools, you will begin to find the seeds of creative design in the technical processes, themselves.

It is possible for the jeweler to develop such an affinity for his work that he takes literal responsibility for its aesthetic worth and for the quality of its craftsmanship. Shown here in the form of a ring is my own personal, registered hallmark, which serves as my signature, trademark and seal, and which has evolved through five previous ring forms to reach its present state.

The ring itself has been executed in what I call a plasto-graphic style, which is a difficult style to verbalize. To describe it in a literal manner is antipathetical to its very nature. For it is a style that is generally composed

The author's registered hallmark used as the motif for a ring (1965).

18

Designs for rings including one for two fingers.

Opposite: Sterling silver ring, centrifugal casting (1964). This was the first ring executed by the author; it was named "Face of the Sun."

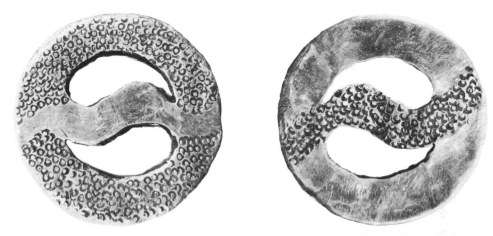

Two views of a sterling silver prototype coin (1967), to be used in consultation with the *I Ching* or *Book of Changes,* an ancient Chinese book of philosophy which can be used for divination. The design on the coin represents the traditional Yin and Yang symbols. Texture was achieved with a texturing tool and chasing hammer (see Chapter 5).

of "solid-line" construction, or of symbols which are unconscious in origin. And since symbols are not definable in literal equivalents, I will not attempt lengthy explanations, but only hope their meanings will speak as eloquently to you as they do to me.

The rings and articles executed in this style are essentially like drawings, graphic devices, or images which have taken on solid form. They are plastic in that they are manifested in a three-dimensional form, and graphic in that they can be rendered as drawings or engravings, or as tablets, frottages, reliefs, etc.

The sources of the symbols are largely unconscious. I approach my materials with little or no concept in mind, in many cases, and depend on the materials themselves to provide a clue to the final image. The hidden ideas lie deep within me, awaiting a vehicle to give them concrete actuality. The roots of this particular style may be apparent only after my work is completed, for I do not generally apprehend it intellectually before that stage.

Sterling silver rings, to be worn as a pair (1967). To achieve a natural sculptured effect reminiscent of excavated "rock tablets," irregular textures were applied to the wax models. After the rings were cast, unsuitable textures were removed and selected surfaces polished (see Chapter 5).

I often find a sculptural influence in this mode of working. Many times I have perceived the finished article in a manner that would indicate its effectiveness as a large-scale object. For example, note the photographs of the pair of rings called "Rock Tablet Rings." I envisioned these rings as huge, roughhewn rock tablets standing on a barren, rocky hillside or plateau. Not all of the articles in this style, however, lend themselves to such a large-scale disposition.

Often, I create in a third style by assembling symbolic elements in such profusion that they appear to be almost organic or mechanical in their nature. The result, manifested in a bas-relief, may be seen in the accompanying photographs. These complex compositions first evolved from simple drawings through which I began to understand the effect of chiaroscuro in

Above: Sterling silver ring, centrifugal casting (1968). Note how the individual units are arranged in a conglomerate to form the mass of the object. *Right:* A visual analogy is drawn between the component parts of the ring and natural forms.

Sterling silver ring (1964). This marks the author's first effort to create jewelry as an art form rather than pure decoration.

regard to solid form. This has been of enormous aid to me in understanding the relationships of colors in metals and stones and their influence upon design. It has also aided me in realizing concepts of space.

I have developed a fourth style in my work, which appears to be quite literal and generally representational in outward appearance. The forms are closely related to the symbolic ones, although they are at first look of a different nature. When I previously mentioned unconscious elements in styles, I omitted any mention of the emergence of archetypal symbols or themes which are thought by some to be common in the collective experience of all men and from which these elements are drawn.

Linear and organic designs for gravures or enamels.

22

Group of three rings: *left to right*—Sterling silver ring composed of four interrelated linear forms (1968); sterling silver ring, set with a 30-carat carnelian oval (1967) (see page 60); sterling silver ring (1966). These rings are executed in the plasto-graphic style, characterized by a series of molded "solid-line" forms. Differences in the initial wax models (from which the rings were cast) and methods of finishing make each ring unique.

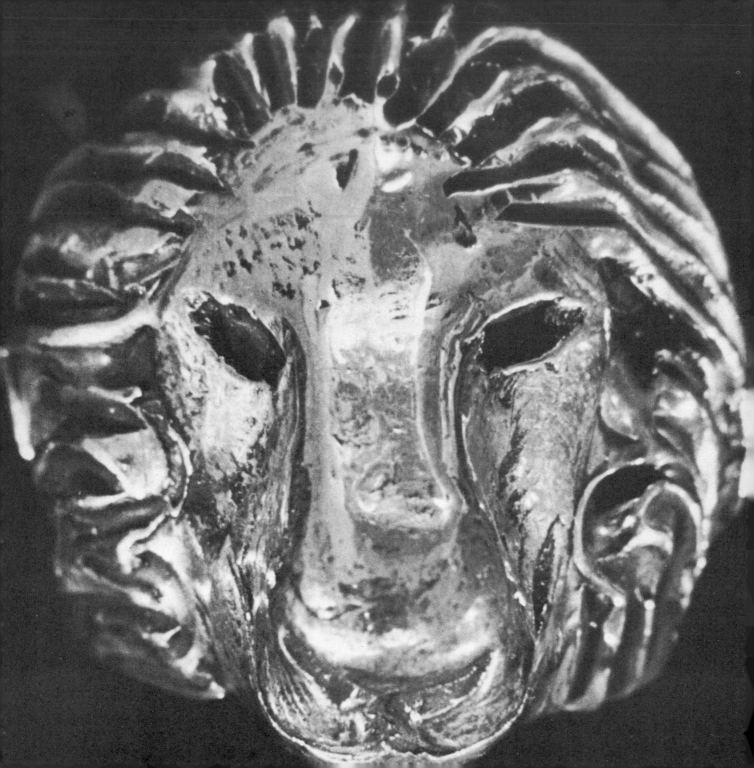

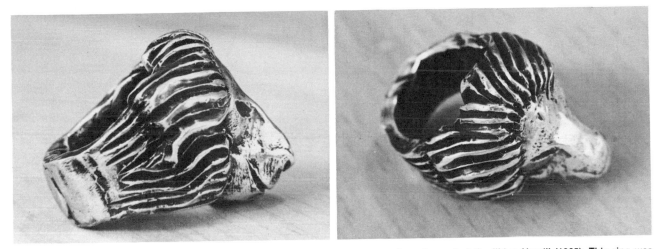

Opposite and above: Three views of a sterling silver ring called the "Lion Head" (1965). This ring was modeled in beeswax using the additive process: the individual forms were shaped first and then joined together with a heated bonding tool (see Chapter 3).

Artists in various fields of artistic endeavor throughout the ages have attempted to be deliberately unique with thematic material. Many of these artists have completed a work which they considered to be totally original only to discover that the nearly identical article, theme, style, or symbol had already been created by someone else, either earlier or simultaneously. The very first ring I ever made pleased me greatly until, months later, while looking through a seventy-five year old book dealing with Egyptian antiquities, I discovered that the ring was exactly the same in every detail save one — size — as an Egyptian ring dating from the time of Amenhotep III. I

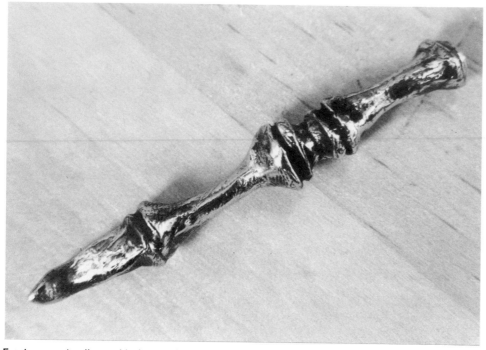

Fourteen-carat yellow gold pipe smoker's pick and tamp tool (1966). This was modeled in beeswax and many impressions applied in the wax model were left after the casting process, enhancing the fossil-like form of the piece.

studied the phenomenon further and found that the experience is not that uncommon, as parallels in the study of art history bear out.

Whatever the cause, pieces in this fourth style are more readily assimilated than many of the symbolic objects because they are much more representational. Nonetheless, they are symbols and, due to this fact, it is difficult to convey their personal meaning in words.

MATERIALS

3

Spontaneity has become an important element in my method of work through the use of the technique of lost-wax casting. This technique provides the opportunity to escape the pitfalls of hard-edged design which can inhibit the creative potential of jewelry making.

All of the objects that I cast are first fashioned by hand in wax in all of their exact detail. Since wax is often in a pliable, workable state, it lends itself to the immediacy of creative expression. Often, you will discover methods of applying textures, or will create new textures accidentally. The important thing to remember, however, is that you must be selective about what is to remain in the finished object.

The first wax which I suggest you try is refined beeswax. This wax is rather pliable at a temperature slightly higher than that of average room temperature. This makes it ideal for the beginner to experiment with in the early stages of model making or designing. It is, however, one of the most difficult waxes to work with successfully because of its pliability. You must, while allowing this material to suggest form, control it and shape it to the desired contours. Currently, I am using waxes of approximately six different

Opposite: Wax model of a belt buckle, later cast in jeweler's bronze (1968). Note the fingerprints in the surface of the wax. These were retained and transformed into metal because they proved to be compatible with the creative concept of the object.

Shown here are three stages of constructive wax working. From a quantity of pliable beeswax, individual forms are made, then assembled.

hardnesses in the making of models. Frequently, I blend various waxes to obtain certain qualities which cannot be had in any of the prepared waxes. By experimentation you can determine which waxes work most successfully for you.

Left: Wax model for a six-legged ring (1966). *Right:* Wax setting for a 20-carat watermelon tourmaline. The bezel is constructed in a mixture of beeswax and dental inlay wax, and will be refined after the piece is cast.

I suggest, also, that this is a good manner in which to learn design and "solid sketching" techniques. By working with wax, you avoid making errors that can be very costly when executed in precious metals. As your skill with this material grows, you will be able to determine by a finished wax what the article will look like when transformed into metal.

Wax model for finger ring (1968). Note the fingerprints in the surface of the wax. The casting process allows for exact reproduction of such textures, and during the finishing process the jeweler can decide what is to remain. The small forms of this ring were executed directly with the hand.

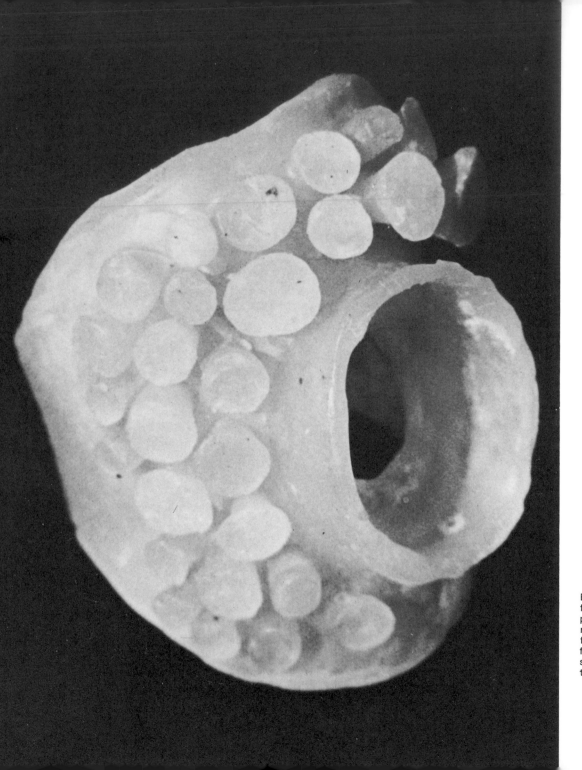

Beeswax model for a "growing form" variety of ring. Textures applied to the wax model should be refined as much as possible before the article is cast, although final, selective removal of undesired surfaces can be made after the casting process.

After the wax is fashioned, all possible constructions or devices necessary to the finished article (which can be cast) should be articulated. Bezels for stones, or prongs and suspension devices, as in the case of a pendant, should be included whenever possible. Construct the required forms and, by means of heated tools, "wax solder" them in the correct place to secure the construction. You can render the forms by modeling the wax with your hands and by articulating it with what are basically dental tools designed for wax working.

Wax working tools. Left to right: alcohol lamp, scalpel, dental pick, vehe pick, probe, tweezers.

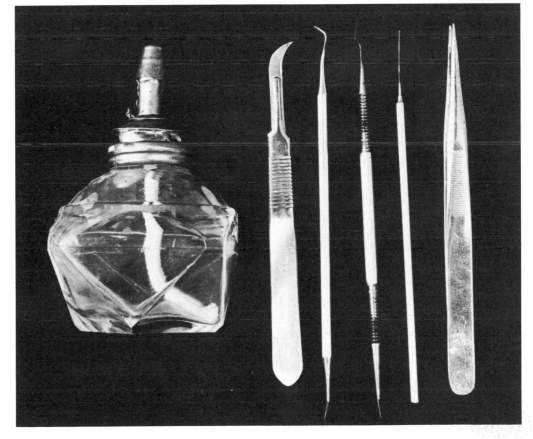

Left: Carved wax ring (1968). The form was carved with a scalpel from a block of hard casting wax. Blade marks are eliminated with a torch flame. *Center:* Carved wax setting (1967). Here, space is utilized fully by opening the mass to the passage of light. *Right:* A carved wax design for a ring (1966).

Apart from the additive process, which is begun with the basic construction of the desired form, there is also the subtractive process. Using this process, you remove from a block of wax of considerable hardness all that is necessary to reveal the form. You use the wax tools as chisels and, much as in the classical method, sculpt form from where it did not previously exist. The wax most commonly used in this process is called "hard, green, casting wax." This is not to be confused with "hard injection wax," which, although sometimes employed for carving, is generally used to fill a mold in order to recast a piece that has been previously executed.

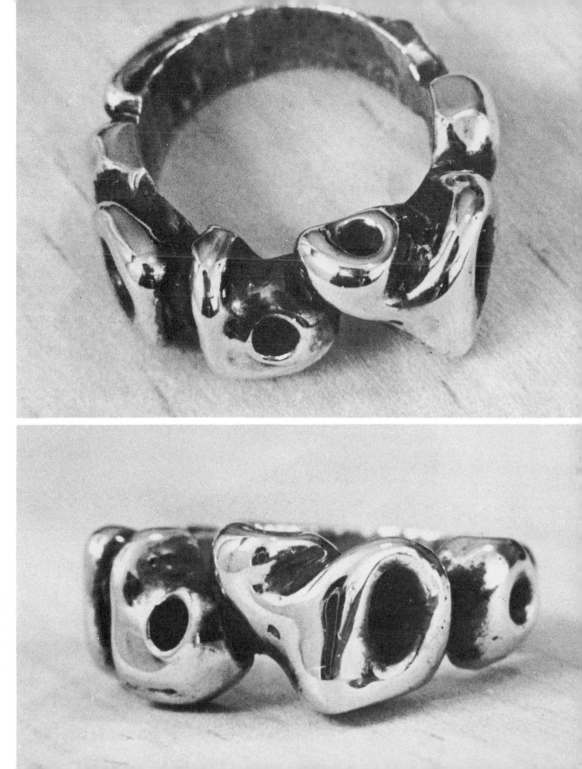

Two views of a 14-carat gold carved ring (1965). In this example of the subtractive process of modelling, a scalpel was employed like a chisel to carve the form out of a block of hard green casting wax. This method of removing from a block of wax all that is necessary to reveal form is closely related to the classical method of sculpting marble.

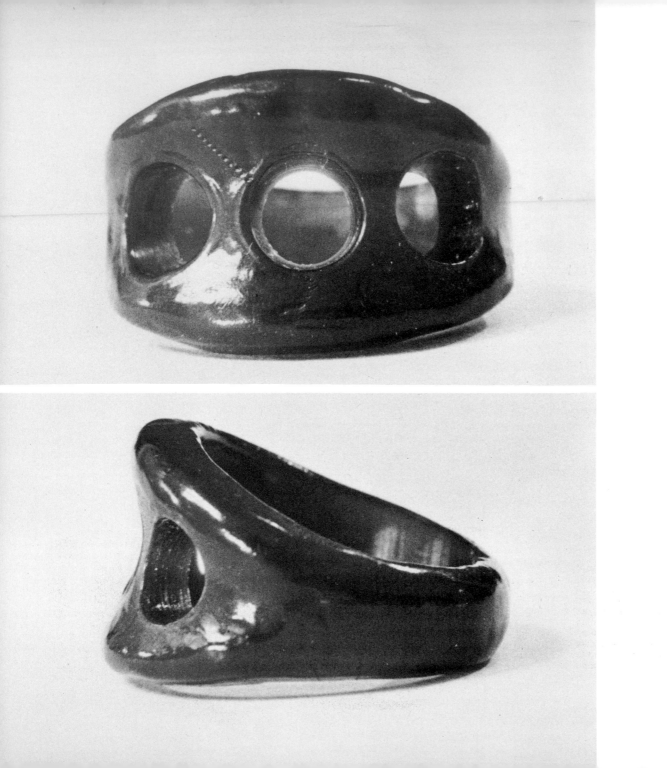

Sterling silver solid-line ring (1966). An example of the additive process of hand modeling. Separate units of this ring were first shaped out of softened, pliable beeswax and then assembled with a heated bonding tool.

To use the additive form of modeling, start with a quantity of wax that has been softened with the aid of an alcohol lamp, or other heat source, and work it with the hands until pliable. Then, shape quantities of the material into their respective forms and join where necessary with a heated bonding tool.

Often, you will find it necessary to combine the additive and subtractive processes.

Only with wax can you really exert the "direct" touch of your hands (via casting the model) upon metal. By contrast, when working directly with metal, you cannot shape and mold with your fingers, nor immediately feel the form which you wish to create. Wax is invaluable for its capacity to allow immediate contact with the birth of form.

Achieving a clean, finished style in wax working is a matter of practice and skill. The hard-edged style can also be executed through proper handling of the wax.

It is of interest to note that most of the present-day waxes successfully used in the casting process have been developed not by the jewelry industry, but by the dental profession in their effort to provide people with well-articulated artificial dentures. The technical aspects of casting have been advanced greatly in the jeweler's favor as a by-product of dental research and science.

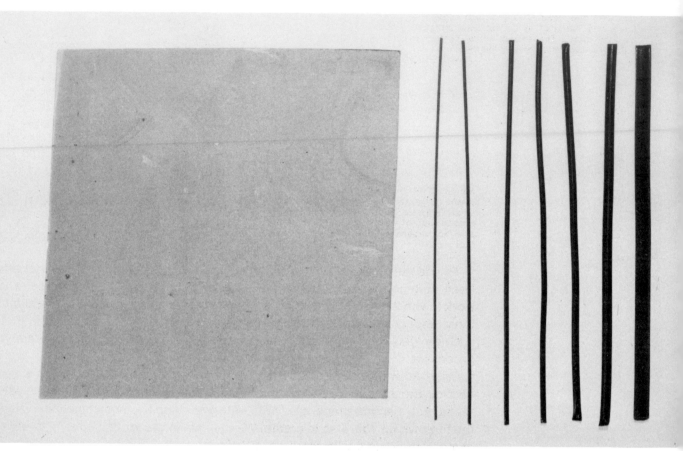

Commercially prepared waxes are available in a variety of hardnesses and preshaped forms.

The metals most commonly associated with the making of jewelry are silver, gold and platinum. These are the "noble" or "precious" metals. They are so-called because of certain innate properties which make them suitable for use as attractive objects. These metals all have a particular beauty that sets them apart from what we have come to call the "baser" metals.

Prepared waxes may be purchased in sheets, rods, blocks, and other shapes. Shown here are a few of the hundreds of prepared forms available.

Gold was, perhaps, the first metal used by man. Its pure, or 24-carat, state was relatively easy to work with, and it could, therefore, be fashioned by means of pounding and beating. For centuries, in its pure state, it was made into an infinite variety of objects for wear. It is only a relatively recent achievement, however, that has made gold a sturdy, as well as a beautiful, metal, either for wearing or working.

One half ton of rocks yields approximately ½ ounce of the refined metal. Gold has a specific gravity of 19.3, making it one of the densest metals on earth. Pure gold melts at a temperature of 1,063° C. When alloyed, its melting temperature is variable, depending upon the metals added. The melting point of pure gold on the Fahrenheit scale of temperature is 1,945.4°.

Pure gold is said to contain 24 carats, or parts, of gold, and 0 parts of any other metal. It follows, then, that 22-carat gold contains 22 parts of gold and 2 parts of another metal; 18-carat gold contains 6 parts of another metal; 14-carat gold, 10 parts of another metal; 10-carat gold, 14 parts of another metal. Gold is alloyed and identified according to the amount of pure gold contained within the alloy. Pure gold (24-carat) is too soft to be used successfully in the making of jewelry. It is of beautiful color and is aesthetically pleasing, but would, with normal wear, scratch, bend, and wear down at an alarming rate. The setting of stones in 24-carat gold is possible but not at all practical.

The following chart contains the approximate percentages of pure gold contained in the listed carat weight metals:

24-carat gold	100%	pure
22 " "	91.67%	pure
18 " "	75%	pure
14 " "	58.5%	pure
10 " "	41.67%	pure

Gold is available commercially in a variety of colors as well as carats and forms. Among the most popular are yellow, white, pink (or red) and green.

These colors are the result of alloying gold with other metals. For example, white gold was developed to replace the more costly platinum. In most cases, white gold is produced by alloying pure gold in correct proportion with sterling silver, nickel and zinc. There are a number of accurate ways in which the color can be made white without sacrificing the workability of gold, or the desired color, but the carat value of the gold must be maintained. It matters little what the other parts of the finished alloy are, for its value is based strictly on its gold content. However, the properties of the added metals must be carefully weighed and understood for a usable metal to be produced.

White gold can have a percentage breakdown of metals as follows:

	Gold	Sterling	Copper	Zinc	Nickel
14 carat	58.5%	22.4%	14.1%	5%	—
18 carat	75 %	0 to 20%	—	8 to 20%	4 to 10%

Other colors of gold can be obtained by amalgamating different metals. Red, pink, or rose colored gold can be obtained by alloying with copper; green gold can be made by alloying 19 parts gold with 5 parts silver, or by adding cadmium. Blue gold can be made by alloying 18 parts gold with 6 parts iron; purple gold, by adding 6 parts aluminum to 18 of gold. A lovely shade of lilac gold can be obtained by adding 25-30% zinc. Unfortunately, this last alloy, however lovely to the eye, has proven to be unworkable.

There are a number of factors to consider in deciding whether or not to use gold. Expense is definitely one of these, as gold is at least ten times as costly as silver. An aesthetic judgment is also essential: whether or not to use stones, for example, and whether or not gold is the best metal to be used in terms of the design, purpose, function, weight and mass of the proposed object.

Generally speaking, for the beginner and for the advanced jeweler, silver provides an exciting medium of expression. Its color is attractive and its malleability is unequalled. Silver does tarnish, however, due to various sulfides in the air, or acids within the system of the wearer, but, on the whole, it is truly a noble metal with which to work.

Silver has a specific gravity of 10.5, a low melting point (961° C. and 1,729.8° F.), takes a high polish, and is well suited for use in the setting of stones. Sterling silver has become the standard for silver jewelry throughout most of the world. It consists of 925 parts fine silver to 75 parts of another metal. In most cases, the alloy used is copper. This alloy gives silver a hardness, not to be found in pure silver, that is necessary for its practical use in jewelry.

Silver has a particular beauty of its own and, although it is less valued in our present age, to some ancient civilizations it was more highly revered than gold.

Platinum is the most costly and dense of the metals normally used in jewelry production. It has not decreased in popularity even though white gold has been successfully developed and marketed throughout the world. Platinum has a density of 21.43, and an enormously high melting point (1,773° C. or 3,223.4° F.) in comparison with silver or gold. This high melting point, combined with extremely high cost (approximately $9.80 per dwt.), places it out of the realm of use for many professionals as well as amateurs. Pure platinum is also too soft to be used without alloying. Five per cent of another metal is sufficient to correct this condition, and 10% iridium makes it a very hard, durable metal with which to work. Platinum is generally used to hold diamonds. I have never seen it used without a stone, or with anything less than a gem quality stone, although that does not prevent its having other uses. Again, cost is probably the controlling factor and, as platinum is not as reflective as silver or white gold, you must exercise a personal choice about the intrinsic value of a metal in determining whether or not to use it.

The weight of precious metal is designated by the troy system of measure. Those units which most concern the jeweler are the pennyweight and the ounce. Pennyweight is often abbreviated to dwt., the letter "d" being the same literal abbreviation used in the English system of pounds, shillings, pence, etc. In the troy system, 20 dwts. are equal to 1 ounce. The simple base is the grain, which equals 0.0648 grams in the metric scale. Twenty-four grams equal 1 dwt., 20 dwts. equal 1 ounce, 12 ounces equal 1 pound. Carat stones are measured by the same system. One carat is equal to 3.086 grains.

Beginning jewelers often confuse the weight and the mass of a metal. Since it is less dense than the other precious metals, an ounce of silver provides more metal than does an ounce of platinum or of gold.

Copper, iron, aluminum, pewter and a number of nonprecious metals which have been specifically developed to take the place of gold can be occasionally useful as a source of cheap material with which to work out designs. However, results may not be as satisfactory in these materials as in the more "noble metals." Familiarizing yourself with the natures of the different materials will help you to develop sound and sensitive aesthetic and technical judgments and to render your ideas in the best possible way.

Copper is a rich-looking metal with a specific gravity of 8.9 (slightly less dense than silver). It has a melting point of 1,083° C. or 1,949.4° F. It can be wrought and soldered well, and is excellent for casting if alloyed into bronze. Copper with 8 to 10% tin as an alloy is known as bronze. Many jewelers work in a metal commonly known as "jeweler's bronze." Gold, silver, and copper in their pure forms are the most ductile metals with which to work. They are highly malleable, and can be shaped in mass or drawn into fine wires.

On occasion, you may encounter a material called German silver. This substance was developed many years ago in China and is, in reality, copper alloyed with zinc and nickel. German silver is about as workable as brass. Although at first glance its color appears to be similar, it does not actually have the superior finish of silver.

By adding approximately 17% zinc to copper, you can produce a gold colored metal with reasonably good working properties, which is rather like the kind of metal known as pinchbeck. Pinchbeck was developed over two hundred years ago by a man named Christopher Pinchbeck, to serve as an economical substitute for yellow gold. A material called Nu-Gold, which is similar to pinchbeck, is available through various craft suppliers. (See list of suppliers for materials.)

METHODS

4

As you develop familiarity with the different methods of shaping jewelry, you can determine more readily which technique will best facilitate different designs. I use the casting technique more than the handwrought method because I find that it allows me more freedom. For example, I can reshape a wax model innumerable times with far less expenditure of effort than if I were designing directly in metal.

Casting is a fascinating process, reminiscent of alchemy, and it is difficult to become involved in it without finding yourself occupied with all the aesthetic imagery that the method is capable of producing. Technically, it is not a difficult process. There are available numerous machines that take most of the difficulty out of the lost-wax casting procedure. One of these is the centrifugal casting machine, which is constructed of steel and driven by an internal spring device which, when released, forces molten metal into a previously prepared "ring" or "flask."

If you use the lost-wax process, you "sprue" the wax model with wax rods, much as in the wax modeling methods. After the sprues are attached

Spring-driven, broken-arm centrifugal casting machine. The white object on the right end of the arm is the crucible; the flask, or ring, is placed directly behind it. At the right is an adjustable weight. The triggering device is at the top of the base.

Casting accessories. Top row: flasks; bottom row: tongs, sprue bases, clamps, and small tongs.

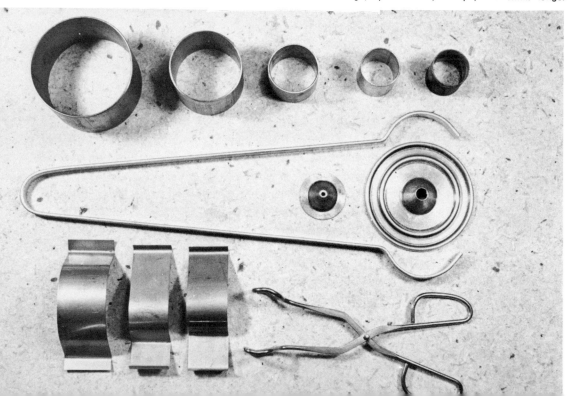

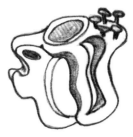

Designs for rings of a sculptural nature, well suited to the lost-wax method of casting.

Sterling silver ring for the ring-finger, set with a 15-carat Persian turquoise (1967). Note the amount of texture applied indirectly to this "growing form" ring through the lost-wax casting process.

Wax-eliminating oven. Large flask and small flask are inside.

for the venting of gasses and for the flow of metal, mount the wax model on a stand or cone which will support it in the flask. Next, brush on a substance much like plaster of Paris in a thin suspension (called "investment") over the entire surface of the wax model and sprues. This should be applied with great care to see that no air bubbles are trapped between the wax and the investment. Having accomplished this, allow the plaster to dry slightly so that the entire model may be checked for error in coverage. Then, if the coating has been sufficiently applied in the correct manner, insert the wax in the flask and pour the same material over the entire wax assembly so that the flask is full of the plaster and so that the sprues are in the correct position for the entry of the metal and the venting of hot gasses. Allow the entire unit to set and dry.

When the drying is completed, place the flask for 45 to 55 minutes in a wax eliminating oven, which has been preheated to the temperature of 1,800° F. This oven is especially constructed for wax eliminating, and kilns of the variety used in the making of pottery should not be used. In the time that passes, constant high heat will totally eliminate the wax and all of its residues and gasses. During the final minutes of the wax elimination, prepare the centrifugal casting machine for the actual casting.

Insert a specially made graphite or clay crucible into the device of the machine and place in the crucible metal pellets of the same material as the article being cast. This metal generally comes in round or nearly round "shot" form, and is clean and newly refined to eliminate impurities that would ruin the cast. When the wax has been thoroughly eliminated, only a hollow mould of investing material will remain within the flask.

To produce the positive of the desired shape, attach the flask to the casting machine in the place provided for it. Tense the machine spring by winding the arm around as many times as it will wind and check the locking device to avoid a premature activation of the spring. Bring the crucible in contact with the flask at the correct angle and melt the metal by applying a heavy torch flame to the crucible.

When the metal has become molten, the triggering device will release to allow the spring to unwind and the arm of the machine to swing freely in its orbit around the base. At this point, the molten metal will be propelled by centrifugal force into the hollow portions of the plaster investment mould. If the quantity of metal is sufficient to fill the volume of the mould, if the metal has been brought to the proper state of liquidity, and, barring error in the process of investment, if the wax has been thoroughly eliminated, you may remove the flask with tongs and plunge it into warm water for cooling. The flask will generally be very hot and contact with the water will cause the plaster to crack so that the object with its sprues can be removed with relative ease. You may then remove the sprues with a heavy sprue cutter and, unless there has been an error in the steps along the line to the actual casting, the object produced will be exact, even in minute detail, to the wax model.

As with all endeavors, practice makes the results progressively better.

Through repeated attempts, you will master the technique, and your unsuccessful attempts at employing this method will occur with diminished frequency.

In certain circles, casting has come to be regarded as a means of mass production rather than as a means of bringing a single unique work into being. I believe that this viewpoint prevails because the casting process has proved itself applicable to that end and not because it is primarily a technique developed for the purpose of mass reproduction. I am sure that Benvenuto Cellini did not think in terms of mass production when he brought into solidity a piece of his famous work by means of the lost-wax procedure. Cellini was quite involved with this process, and numerous fine examples of his work will attest to the beauty of unique objects either totally or partially produced by this technique.

The handwrought approach is also essential to the creation of form for the jeweler. It is by this means that castings are finished and objects created directly in metal. When working with this technique, you will find there is little room for error, because the effect of the error is witnessed immediately in the material. Since the metals of the craft are much more difficult to work with than wax, and since metal is so much more costly, you should first perfect your techniques in a cheaper medium. Copper is of moderate cost and an excellent material for this purpose.

Designs for complicated rings, including some with gypsy-set stones.

Basic jeweler's tools. Left to right: Jeweler's saw frame and blades, four basic needle files, chasing hammer, rawhide mallet, flat file, rattail file, triangular file, ring file (½" round), charcoal block, needle-nosed pliers, flux brush, oxygen-gas torch (noke type), ring mandrel, tinner's snips, chasing tool, crosslock tweezer, ring sizes, asbestos block.

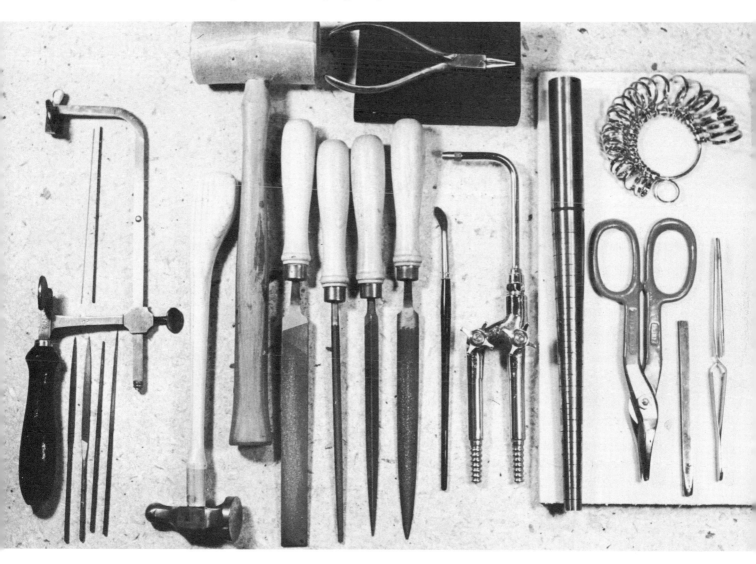

Essentially tools for working directly in metal are the following:

1. Asbestos block — 12″ square, ¼″ to ½″ thick — To protect bench surface from heat during soldering operations.

2. Charcoal Block — Approximately 4″ x 5″ x 2″ — To reflect heat back to the object being soldered.

3. Torch — (Or other suitable source of high heat.) All soldering or joining operations are accomplished by the application of heat. Air-gas, or oxygen-gas torches are the best means.

4. Small Camel's-hair Brush — To apply flux to surfaces that are to be soldered.

5. Files — half-round, round, and flat or medium cut. — To shape smooth surfaces.

6. Jeweler's Saw Frame and Blades — To cut sheets, rods, and other metal materials into desired shapes.

7. Rawhide Mallet — A mallet of rolled rawhide — To be used for forming metal without marking its surface.

8. Tweezers — To transfer solder to the desired area and to hold pieces in place while soldering, etc.

9. Roundnosed Pliers — To aid in forming bends in wire, and for bezels, etc.

10. Tinner's Snips (Metal Shears) — To cut sheets of metal and wire to desired shape or length.

11. Bench Pin, or V-Board — A piece of hardwood shaped like a wedge, with a V-shaped cut in the end, which acts as a third hand to support and to hold work while it is being cut, filed, or drilled.

12. Needle Files — Small files (about 6″ in length) of No. 2 cut — To articulate curves and areas of difficult access.

13. Scotch Stone — To remove scratches from the surfaces of metals.

14. Brightboy Eraser — A composition of abrasives used to remove scratches from the surfaces of metals.

15. Buff Stick — A stick upon which felt or leather is mounted, which, when impregnated with tripoli or rouge, is used to polish metals. (This is an adequate but time consuming method of polishing work and should be employed only when a polishing lathe is not available.)

16. Ring Mandrel — To shape ring sizes, forms, etc.

There are at least two hundred other noteworthy tools used by the professional jeweler to assist in the creation of handwrought jewelry. As a beginner, however, you will find that well-made objects can be fashioned with these essential tools.

In all soldering operations, hard solders are used. Soft solder or lead solder is not compatible with the needs of the craftsman dealing with precious metals. A hard solder is a solder made of the same material as the metals to be joined (normally) but alloyed to melt at a melting point which is lower than that of the connecting pieces. You can, therefore, melt the solder and unite it to the other metal without endangering work in progress. In multiple soldering operations, you may perform subsequent solderings with solders of lower melting points. In this way, you need not worry about previously made joints coming apart.

Soldering is a necessary technique to learn if you wish to produce any reasonably complex piece of work. It is accomplished by applying heat to the parts which are to be joined so that the solder melts and forms a bond between the parts. It is most important to remember that the pieces to be joined must fit as closely as possible so that the solder, when reduced to a molten state, will fill the smallest possible space and create a firm bond. The metal to be joined must be clean and free from foreign materials, or the solder will not fill the desired space. Flux, which is a preparation applied to the area where solder is to flow, is intended to keep the area free from oxidation so that the solder will bond in the desired place in the intended manner. A variety of hard solder fluxes are available from craft and

Fourteen-carat yellow gold ring and matching bracelet (1965). Both pieces were first designed in fused wax-wire and then cast. Using abstract, free-form designs is an extremely useful way to learn the potentialities of positive and negative space and the mechanics of mass.

trade suppliers and the craftsman should not hesitate to experiment with a number of them to find the preparation which best fulfills his needs.

For silver solder to flow correctly, the entire mass of metal must be heated uniformly. In the bonding of gold, the area to be heated may be localized around the desired joint.

Silver and gold solders come in a variety of forms and melting points. These melting points are designated by the terms "easy," "medium," and "hard." An easy solder flows at a lower temperature than does a medium or a hard solder. If you are using more than one kind of solder on a given piece of jewelry, you should identify each so that after performing an initial soldering operation you do not subsequently ruin that joint by using another solder which requires greater heat. Additional heat will cause the easier flowing solder to remelt and thereby destroy the first bond.

If you create an object through the handwrought technique, you should cut your metals to the desired shapes, form them with the tools at your disposal, assemble them by means of soldering, and finish them as you would if you were working on a casting that had just been freed from the investment. A discussion of the basic finishing techniques and the aesthetics thereof appears later in the book.

Why should you choose casting as a technique? There are a number of reasons quite apart from the aesthetics which are also involved with the process. First and foremost, it is more economical to make patterns and designs in wax. Second, the tools with which wax patterns are executed can be improvised. When you seek to make a solid object out of an intangible idea, you learn, in pursuit of that idea, the correct method and means of revealing desired form. Through the discovery of how to adapt materials to needs, you begin to understand the functions of professional tools and to advance in the techniques of modeling. The value of pursuing proficiency in a modest way lies in thoroughly exploring the limits of your abilities while you are working with basic materials. In this way, you do not become confused by the alternatives presented in a profusion of equipment and supplies. These alternatives may, at the beginning stages of work, prevent your developing a personal and meaningfully evolved style. Through the process of observation, you reach a kind of objectivity. Casting reveals transforma-

Fourteen-carat gold man's wedding band, centrifugal casting (1968). To make this ring, a series of interrelated forms were constructed in wax in ring form. Then a thin membrane of wax was applied to the inside of the form. When the ring was cast, a thin gold band backing the forms was left. The outside surface was then highly polished to create an overall solidity of form.

Fourteen-carat yellow gold wedding band, set with twenty-three .04-carat round white diamonds (1966). This ring was executed directly in metal by traditional hand-wrought methods. The diamonds were set with four tiny beads per stone.

Sterling silver index-finger ring, centrifugal casting (1967). This ring is set with a natural corundum ruby of deep brown-red color, sometimes called a plum sapphire. This was cut *en cabochon* (rounded and domed), so that entering light creates three intersecting rays of light—a six-pointed star (asterism)—within the stone. (The asterism is unfortunately photographically unreproducible.) This unique aspect of the stone influenced the design of the setting. The rays were used as a point of departure for the six major forms which grow from the bezel. The remaining, smaller forms were added as subdivisions of the remaining spaces.

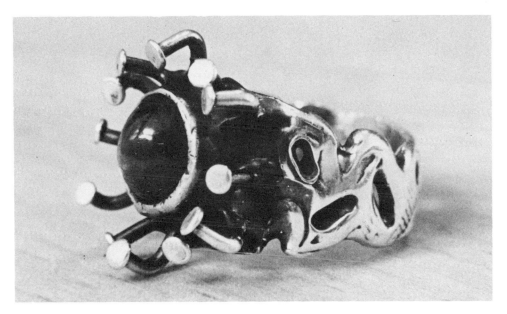

tions and, as you increase your capacity to recognize these, you can alter and develop the objective quality of your work, and progress along with it.

Occasionally, for aesthetic and technical reasons, I render something by the handwrought process. I use this technique to create an evolved form, i.e., either an object which, through a series of previous pieces, has "shed" its more obvious organic or symbolic characteristics or an object which must possess a highly finished or refined character.

The handwrought process lends itself so well to precision results that it is indispensable to the jeweler as a means to accomplish an end. Nevertheless, the technique which is best is the technique that is, in your judgment, most capable of communicating the design concept you have in mind.

A stone can contain the aesthetic impetus that gives rise to a concept of design. The rings shown in the photographs are examples of this.

The ruby is asterated (it contains a six-rayed star of light) and was formed by the inclusion of "silk" within the nearly opaque plum-colored corundum (in this case, ruby). When the stone was cut *en cabochon* (rounded and

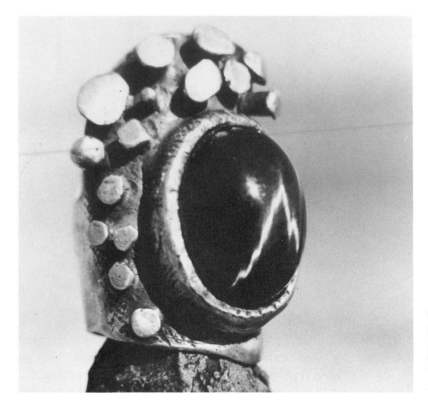

Sterling silver ring for the little-finger (1967). The gypsy-set stone is a 25-carat blue tigereye (quartz variety), which contains a chatoyancy—a narrow band of light that moves across the surface of the stone as its position changes. The shifting color and constant play of light and shadow produced by the chatoyant quality in the tigereye determined the "growing form" design of the ring.

domed, as opposed to the facets used in transparent or nearly transparent stones), the entering light created three intersecting rays of light — or a six pointed star within the stone. In reality, these are three intersecting lines. Using the six extremities of the star and the median points between them, a setting was constructed so that the effect of the finished article is one of a well-integrated whole.

The blue tigereye stone contains a narrow band of light which moves across its surface as its position shifts. This property, called chatoyancy, creates a constant play of light and shadow in the stone. The ever-changing color and luster of the tigereye determined the organically oriented design of the ring.

In the beginning, do not be overly concerned with stones. As your technique and design-making capacities grow, you will become aware of the myriad possibilities offered by the use of stones in the making of designs.

Aside from such considerations as shape, size, cost, and color, the structural properties of stones must also be evaluated.

The diamond is the hardest substance on earth. On the Moh's scale, it has a hardness of 10. The next ranking stone is the corundum, which includes all forms of the sapphire and ruby, with a hardness of 9. The difference in hardness between the diamond and the corundum as evidenced by the Moh's scale is 1 unit. In reality, the diamond is approximately 90 times harder than the corundum. The Moh's scale is primarily useful in that it provides some comparative means by which to judge which stones are of suitable hardness to be used in jewelry.

Fourteen-carat yellow gold ring, centrifugal casting, set with a 3.5-carat opal (1967). This ring has an organic quality because it was created as an extension of the opal (in its own matrix) cut *en cabochon.*

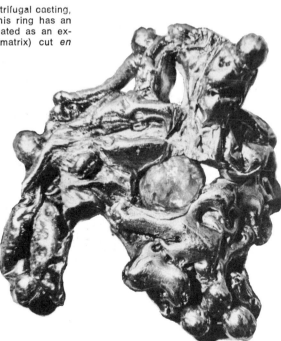

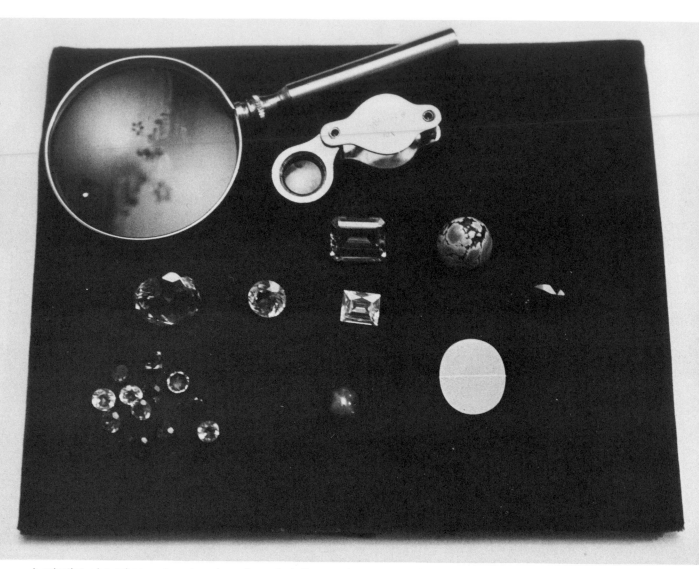

A selection of precious and semi-precious stones including amethyst, star sapphire, ruby, Persian turquoise, peridot, tourmaline, banded agate, rose quartz and topaz. Note the small magnifying tool on the left. It is known as a diamond loop and used extensively in the classification of transparent gemstones.

Sketches for rings well suited to the lost-wax method of casting.

In general, it is unwise to set any stone which has less than a unit rating of 4.5 on the Moh's scale. The hardness of a stone will also, to some degree, dictate the method by which it should be set. For example, it is unwise to set a stone with a hardness of 4.5 to 5.5 in a setting which is not going to provide some degree of protection for the stone. Often, you will find it desirable, from the standpoint of design and practicality, to set a stone in what is know as a hammered, or gypsy, setting. This kind of setting requires that the metal around the stone be filed to reduce its thickness, and then be forced over the edge of the stone by means of a chasing tool and hammer. This kind of setting is extremely effective in holding the stone securely, but requires considerable practice to execute.

In some cases, the gypsy setting may be applied to a stone with what is known as a handwrought bezel. In other cases, a bezel is omitted, and the stone is set within an extension of the shank of the ring, or mass of the object.

Sterling silver ring for the little-finger, set with a 10-carat Burma moonstone, a variety of feldspar (1967). Here, the extraordinarily strong setting and heavy bezel were used in an effort to protect the relatively soft stone, which is rated 6 on Moh's scale.

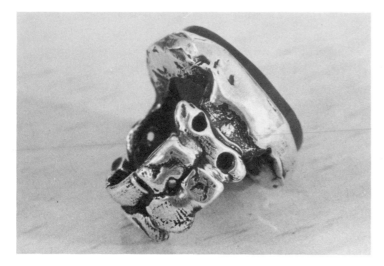

Below: Sterling silver ring, centrifugal casting, gypsy set with a 30-carat carnelian oval (1967). Here, a rather large, plain stone of striking color and dimension is set in a mounting, the shank of which is composed of a series of molded linear forms. *Left:* Detail of the bottom of the shank. Note that the bezel is an extension of the shank itself.

Opposite: Setting a stone in the "gypsy" or hammered method. The metal around the stone has been filed to reduce its thickness, and is being forced over the edge of the stone with a chasing tool and hammer.

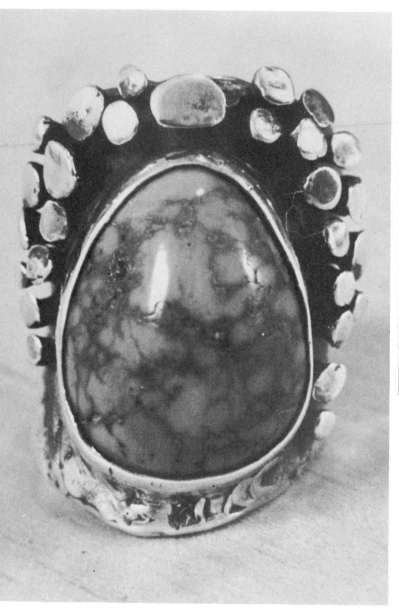

Sterling silver ring for the ring-finger, set with a 15-carat Persian turquoise (1967). Here the stone is gypsy set in a bezel of 30-gauge thickness. All parts of the ring were cast from wax of the same thickness.

Sterling silver index-finger ring, gypsy set with a 7.5-carat Ceylon moonstone. The gypsy setting provides maximum protection for the stone and at the same time allows the stone to play an integrated role in the overall scheme. Note how the bezel is textured to provide an organic environment and how the three domed forms around the outside of the bezel relate to the configuration of the stone itself.

Most of the time, nonprecious stones are set by means of a bezel, which is, readily identified as the topmost part of the ring, or that part of the ring which is seen to hold the stone. The bezel as a device may also be employed on an article other than a ring. For example, the bezel may be soldered to a pin in order to set and display a stone. Often the bezel for a stone is added after the ring or object has been cut. Sometimes the bezel is added to the wax model and cast at the same time as the entire piece and treated as though it were a gypsy mounting.

When you add a bezel to a casting, it is important to use metal of diminished thickness so that it can be manipulated with relative ease after it has been soldered. Some jewelers prefer to use finer quality stock for their bezels, as the metal is then softer and more malleable. A 14-carat gold ring may require a bezel of 16-carat or 18-carat gold to hold the stone. The combination of materials can only be brought about through the use of the handwrought technique. You should deliberate carefully over the requirements of your endeavor before deciding the method and means to employ.

The jeweler, however, is by no means limited to the bezel as a means of setting and securing stones. You may find prongs very effective in setting faceted stones, which are best appreciated when light is allowed to pass through as much of their surface and volume as possible. Transparent or nearly transparent stones are especially suited to the prong setting. These have been cut with facets, as a good diamond is cut, rather than *en cabochon*, as many translucent and opaque stones are cut. What is important is that the prongs be used in harmony with an article so that neither the setting nor the stone are of foremost importance but function entirely together.

Fourteen-carat yellow gold solidline style ring, with semifloral motif, set with a 1.50-carat round white diamond (1967). This ring was designed as a combination wedding ring and engagement ring. The diamond is held firmly in place by four prongs. Prongs, although they appear to be delicate, are perhaps the most effective way of setting fine stones. The beauty of the stone is enhanced by the lyrical movement of lines and negative space surrounding it.

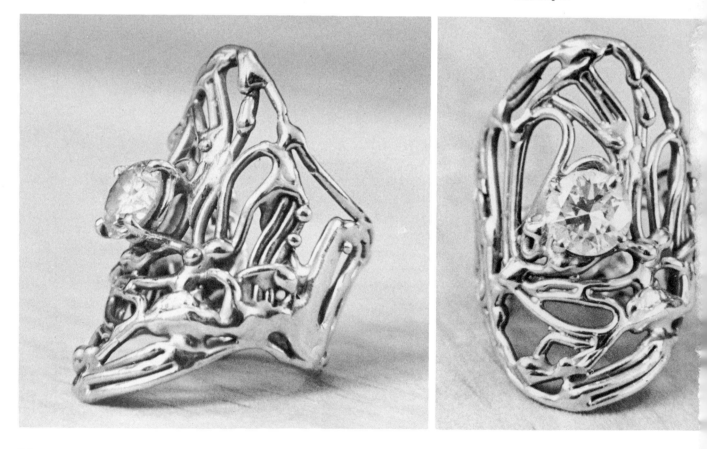

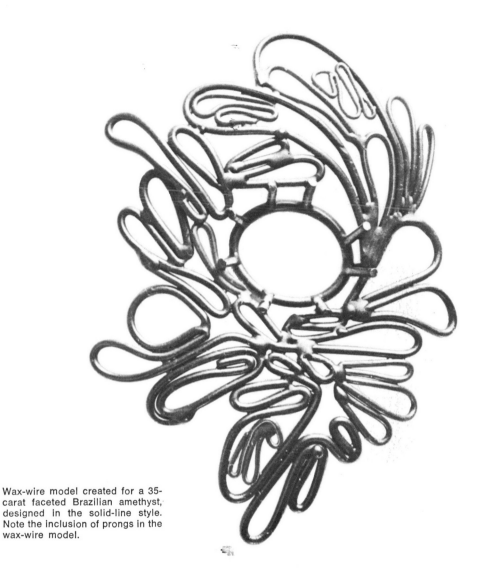

Wax-wire model created for a 35-carat faceted Brazilian amethyst, designed in the solid-line style. Note the inclusion of prongs in the wax-wire model.

Once a design has been created and the area for the stone, or stones, selected, you can solder the prongs into position. Prongs are generally made of wire, tempered to make it less flexible than the wire which is used for any other jewelry making purpose.

You then notch the inside of the prongs so that they will hold the stone around its widest part, or the "girdle," as it is called. The notches should be made in such a way that when the prongs are forced around the stone, the culet, or bottommost part, of the stone will be slightly above the surface of the metal. In some cases, you will find it desirable to have the culet of the stone placed slightly below the surface of the metal, so that the stone does not protrude into space and appear alienated from the mass of the object. In either case, the operation providing for this is called "frasing," which is merely the grinding out of an area directly below the stone and is approximately as large as the volume of the stone from the culet to the girdle. When setting in this manner, you have the opportunity to utilize the concept of negative space. This phenomenon is absent in the bezel or gypsy setting techniques. Here the prongs are arranged around the stone so that the notches hold the girdle firm. The tops of the prongs are then shaped and filed and placed securely over the girdle, or, more specifically, over the template of the stone. The prongs are then polished to remove any rough surfaces.

Four or five well-constructed prongs can hold a stone with maximum security. However, the process is a difficult one, and not recommended for the beginner. There are, in the jewelry profession, qualified setters whose entire business is the execution of such settings. It is therefore wise to give them the actual setting task, unless you are well versed and adept at this kind of construction.

Another effective, but difficult, method of setting stones is the beaded setting technique. Here the stones are placed in a depression in the metal, which has been prepared by frasing, so that the girdle, or girth, of the stone is slightly below the surface of the metal. A tool like a tiny chisel, called a graver (also used in the process of engraving), is then forced into the metal a short distance from the edge of the stone. The graver is pushed toward the stone in one stroke, which raises from the surface a tiny sliver of metal. When the graver is nearly at the edge of the stone, it is raised; with its point used as a fulcrum, it is brought over the top of the stone. This action causes the sliver of metal to curl up over the edge of the stone and to stay in place.

Fourteen-carat gold ring, centrifugal casting, set with 3.5-carat opal (1967). These photographs illustrate in detail how the opal is set. At strategic points, small beads hold the stone securely without detracting from the organic nature of the object as a whole.

A reciprocal action with the graver rounds the top of the sliver, making it appear much like a tiny bead at the edge of the stone.

This beaded setting technique is also very specialized, and requires much practice. I do not recommend it to the beginning jeweler unless the setting is given to a professional for execution.

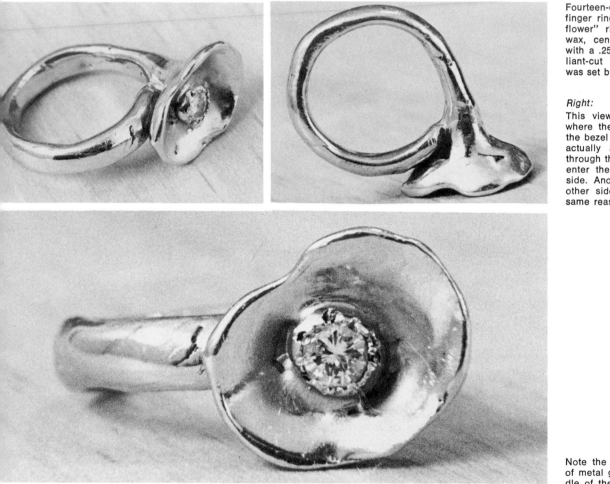

Fourteen-carat yellow gold little-finger ring (1966). This "trumpet-flower" ring was constructed in wax, centrifugally cast, and set with a .25-carat round white, brilliant-cut diamond. The diamond was set by the beading technique.

Right:
This view shows the dark area where the recurved shank meets the bezel of the ring. This area is actually a rectangular slot cut through the metal to allow light to enter the stone from the underside. Another slot is cut on the other side of the shank for the same reason.

Note the small points (or beads) of metal gathered around the girdle of the stone.

FINISHING

5

The finishing of any piece of work is of extreme importance. It is precisely here that you may make an error in judgment which could render the entire effort worthless. However, mistakes can at times be excellent teachers. Freedom to make your own mistakes is important, for it is only through trial and error that your best and most workable techniques will be reached.

At the finishing stages, you must decide exactly what is to remain visible to the eye, and remove all that does not suit your concept of the jewelry. Textures and forms must be prepared to make the entire design function well and to accentuate its best aesthetic qualities. Files, buffs, cutting compounds, grinding and polishing devices are the tools used in finishing. The process of oxidation may also be employed. Through this technique, the reaction of certain chemicals to the surface of the metal may reveal the form of the object with even greater clarity.

After casting or soldering, you must place the article in a solution known as pickling. This is an acid-water solution which removes flux, heat scales, and remaining investment material from the surface of the metal. After a

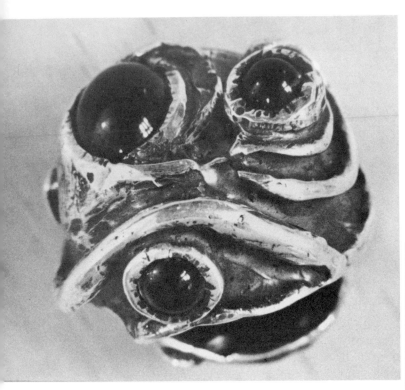

Sterling silver ring, gypsy set with three amethysts (1967). The amethysts are cut *en cabochon*. This massive ring is called the "Greater Magic Tortoise" because the inspiration for its design stemmed from an ancient Chinese myth. Note that on the shank a seemingly representational serpent is articulated. The finishing of this ring was carefully restrained so that random textures could be maintained where they were desirable; these irregular markings and textures can be seen on the finished surface.

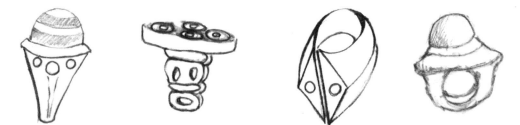

Preliminary sketches for a variety of rings.

piece has been pickled, you must wash it in water to remove the remaining acid solution.

I find that there are many accidental textures which lend themselves beautifully to the nature of the forms with which I work. However, it is only the process of critical selectivity that keeps these textures from going beyond my control. You will find it necessary to appraise your design and to determine that which is enhancing and inherent to its concept and that which is detrimental or detracting. Not all accidental or intended textures are desirable.

For the removal or shaping of metal, the file, in its various combinations, is the primary tool at your disposal. It is the logical extension of your hands when applied to the surface of metal. You can exercise great control over the movements of the file; hence, its function. For the elimination of unwanted textures, such as scratches from the surface of metal, a Scotch stone, or a brightboy eraser, or emery cloths of various grits, can be used.

You can begin the process of polishing with a compound known as tripoli. This is an especially fast cutting compound which is used with a buff on a polishing lathe. It can be applied to gold, silver, copper, etc., and should be employed to cut surface roughness and to provide a preliminary polish before the application of rouge. Once the surface has been prepared through the use of tripoli, and all existing flaws removed, you can polish the metal with rouge. Rouge is a polish only. It has no cutting facility, and it imparts a fine mirror-like shine to the surface when properly applied with a hand buff or a rotary buff on a polishing lathe.

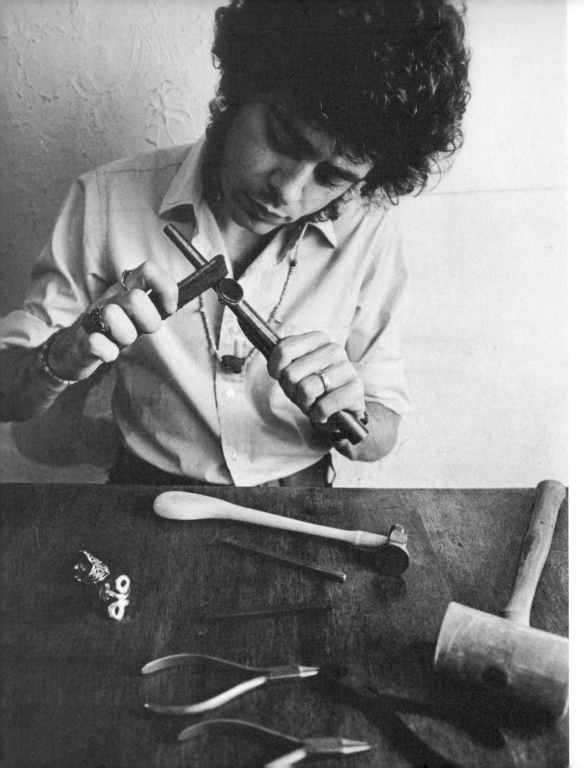

Polishing the bezel surface of a ring by applying tripoli compound by hand with a buff stick. Later, rouge may be applied in the same manner. Tripoli is used to cut the surface roughness and provide a preliminary polish before the application of rouge, which imparts a mirror-like shine to the metal.

Hand polishing is a time consuming but worthwhile procedure. The time spent in appraisal of the total surface of an object during this traditional process is necessary if one is to develop a critical eye and impart to metal a finish that is of the finest quality and appoarance.

Different buffs must be used for each compound. If more than one compound is applied to the same buff, the compounds will not perform their functions successfully. It is also wise to wash the polished article thoroughly between applications of different compounds.

Sometimes you will find it desirable to oxidize the surface of precious metals so that the recessed areas are dark. You then repolish the upper-most areas. In this way, you can better reveal form and create a play of light and shadow that enhances the object and its particular nuances.

Silver is readily oxidized by sulfides in the air. As a jeweler, however, you must have a more controllable means at your service. To oxidize silver, the most commonly used preparation is potassium hydrosulfurate (liver of sulfur). This is a chemical substance which dissolves in heated water. Silver, when dipped into the solution, is darkened almost instantly. This oxidation is merely a surface phenomenon, and has little effect on the metal beyond that. It is important for you to allow an even layer of oxidation (grey-black) to occur before washing off the remaining quantity of the chemical. But leaving metal in the solution too long will build up a layer so thick that the oxidation will have a propensity to flake off. After the article has been thoroughly washed and dried, repolish the surface with rouge to remove the oxidation from all but the recessed areas. You may use powdered pumice for this purpose as well.

Gold will not react to liver of sulfur in the way that silver does. To oxidize gold, a solution containing hydrochloric acid is required. You may apply this to the surface of gold with a small brush, or the object may be dipped. You must heat the gold, however, before oxidation will occur. Be cautious, as this solution is harmful if brought in contact with the skin. You will find a number of these solutions already prepared at any good jeweler's supplier. Do not be concerned with making the solution from "scratch." After the article has been oxidized, it must be washed, dried, and repolished for a finished appearance.

FUTURE OF JEWELRY AS AN ART FORM

Perhaps someday the value of jewelry will be based more on form and artistic merit than on the market value of metal and precious stones. There have been in the past and there are today individual artists whose work within the medium has been accepted and acclaimed even though the materials with which they have dealt have been less than precious. Noted sculptors have executed pieces of unique jewelry — many of them masterpieces — in quite ordinary materials. Their works have been sold at staggering prices. Perhaps someday our more materialistic standards will change to criteria which are predominantly artistic.

I personally believe it is possible for us to transcend the media in which we work and to impart to materials a tiny insight from infinity. I also believe that it is possible for us as individuals to be merely vehicles for a greater force than our own intellectual or technical capacity and that, sometimes in our creative life, we are merely the aperture through which the infinite beauty of the cosmos flows forth, bringing tangible proof of the splendor and inexhaustible variety of experience on all levels. I believe, too, that precious gems and metals are so firmly rooted in the source of creative archetypes that their use and power will never cease, and I also accept the usage of new and different materials which, while they are not "precious," are equally suited to the creation of beautiful jewelry and sculptural art forms.

Perhaps jewelry will embody forms and functions the likes of which we have not yet conceived. Whatever the case, I hope that it offers the opportunity to communicate highly personal experience and development and that through such communication the craft of jewelry making will become an art form of significant meaning and value.

LIST OF SUPPLIERS

JEWELER'S TOOLS

Allcraft Tool and Supply Co., Inc.
22 West 48th Street, New York, N.Y. 10036

Billanti Jewelry Casting Company, Inc.
64 West 48th Street, New York, N.Y. 10036

Gamzon Bros.
15 West 47th Street, New York, N.Y. 10036

Grieger's, Inc.
1633 East Walnut Street, Pasadena, California 91106

Gwinn Craft Supply Company
142 North Market Street, Wichita, Kansas 67202

C. E. Marshall Company
Box 7737, Chicago, Illinois

Wm. J. Orkin, Inc.
373 Washington Street, Boston, Massachusetts 02108

H. Serabian
75 West 45th Street, New York, N.Y. 10036

STONES

A & S Gem and Mineral
611 Broadway, New York, N.Y. 10012

John Barry and Company
Dept. C, P.O. Box 15, Detroit, Michigan

Francis J. Sperisen
166 Geary Street, San Francisco, California 94108

Charles Weidinger
631 West 54th Place, Chicago, Illinois 60609

METALS

Handy & Harmon
82 Fulton Street, New York, N.Y. 10038
330 North Gibson Street, El Monte, California 92000
141 John Street, Toronto, Canada

Southwest Smelting and Refining Company
P.O. Box 2010, Dallas, Texas 75221

INDEX